TAN-GUN
and
TO-SAN

TAN-GUN and TO-SAN

OF TAE KWON DO HYUNG

By JHOON RHEE

Tan-Gun and To-San are two of the hyung required
by the International Tae Kwon Do Federation.

OHARA ⓟ PUBLICATIONS, INCORPORATED
SANTA CLARITA, CALIFORNIA

I would like to express my sincere appreciation to my photographers,
Mr. Jimmy Rudd
And
Mr. Ku Kyung Chung

©1971 Ohara Publications, Incorporated
All rights reserved
Printed in the United States of America
Library of Congress Catalog Card Number 71-150320

Twenty-fourth printing 2003

ISBN 0-89750-001-6

PREFACE

Although introduced only recently in the western world, the art of Tae Kwon Do has become increasingly popular in all countries and with all age groups. Originally conceived in Korea as a measure of unarmed self-defense, Tae Kwon Do has blossomed into an art that is now practiced all over the world.

This book has been written with several purposes in mind. First of all, it is intended to develop a greater appreciation and understanding of Tae Kwon Do, which would contribute toward the growth of this ancient martial art. Since it includes explicit instructions and detailed guidance on all aspects of the art, it will serve as a basic text for beginners. To the intermediate students, this text provides a firm foundation for the more complicated patterns and advanced techniques which follow. It also serves as an authoritative reference on all phases of Tae Kwon Do training for the instructors.

TAN-GUN and TO-SAN is the second in a series of five volumes covering nine of the major hyungs of Tae Kwon Do. The first book dealt with the Chon-Ji hyung required at the white belt level. The two hyungs in this book, Tan-Gun and To-San, are required at the gold belt level. The other books in the series will deal with the remaining hyungs required in order to obtain the black belt.

It is my most sincere wish that this book will embody the true essence of Tae Kwon Do—the discipline and humility which arise from one's dedication to the art. Without such spirit, the student's training is incomplete; with it, he becomes master of himself. For both the physical and spiritual fulfillment of Tae Kwon Do, then, this book is humbly dedicated.

Jhoon Rhee

SENATOR MILTON R. YOUNG
President—U.S. Tae Kwon Do Association

AUTHOR JHOON RHEE

CONTENTS

WHAT IS TAE KWON DO?

Tae Kwon Do is a Korean martial art which has been developed through centuries of Eastern civilization. Today Tae Kwon Do has evolved into not only the most effective method of weaponless self-defense but an intricate art, an exciting sport and a trenchant method of maintaining physical fitness.

Many think that breaking boards and bricks is what Tae Kwon Do consists of, but this is an entirely mistaken concept. Demonstrations displaying such feats merely show the power and speed the human body is capable of utilizing through Tae Kwon Do training.

Tremendous skill and control are required in Tae Kwon Do. While blocking, kicking and punching techniques all contribute to making Tae Kwon Do one of the most exciting and competitive sports, its challenge lies in the adept use of techniques without having any actual body contact. Complete control over punching and kicking movements is paramount in stopping just centimeters short of the opponent.

Through the coordination of control, balance and technique in the performance of hyungs (patterns), Tae Kwon Do is regarded as a beautiful and highly skilled martial art. It is also one of the most all-around methods of physical fitness since it utilizes every single muscle of the body and is considered the ultimate in unarmed self-defense. In Korea, the Presidential Protective Forces are all trained in Tae Kwon Do and several other countries are adopting it into the training programs of their protective forces as well.

WHAT ARE TAE KWON DO HYUNGS?

One of the more important aspects of Tae Kwon Do training is learning Tae Kwon Do hyungs, a set series of attacking and defensive movements which follow a logical, predetermined sequence. Although each hyung comprises different movements or techniques, there are certain basic elements common to all:

1) Each hyung begins and ends from the same point.
2) All movements are performed at speeds and rhythms conforming to those established by the hyungs being performed.
3) All movements must be performed with rapid facing and correct posture.

Each hyung in itself is of immense value in the physical and mental development of the student since it serves many purposes. As a means of physical conditioning, it develops the student's balance, muscle coordination and endurance which ultimately leads to increased self-discipline.

Hyungs also give the student the opportunity to practice the ideal blocking and attacking movements against an imaginary opponent. Just as the student in school learns to print, so his handwriting is a departure from the ideal and becomes a mark of his personal style. The same may be said for Tae Kwon Do. A student's sparring or fighting style becomes his adaptation of the principles he has acquired from hyungs. The hyungs, then, are the student's line between Tae Kwon Do training and actual fighting.

Finally, hyungs are a graphic demonstration of the art of Tae Kwon Do that is a mark of the level of development the student has acquired. As a student progresses he undertakes more complex hyungs. They are designed to challenge and make him call upon his resources and all that he has learned in order to perform the new movements and increase his scope of discipline and development.

Tae Kwon Do hyungs have been developed and perfected throughout the centuries by the outstanding teachers of the art. Each hyung consists of the most logical movements of blocking, punching, striking or kicking possible within that sequence of movements. A student should not attempt to take on a new hyung until he has perfected the hyungs he is required to learn at his level of achievement. Before advancing to another hyung it is customary for a student to perform the one he is presently learning at least 300 times.

WITH WHAT HYUNG
DOES EACH RANK TRAIN?

HYUNG	RANK (Class)	COLOR BELT	AMOUNT PERFORMED
Chon-Ji	10th & 9th	White	At Least 300 Times
Tan-Gun	8th	Gold	At Least 300 Times
To-San	7th	Gold	At Least 300 Times
Won-Hyo	6th	Green	At Least 300 Times
Yul-Kok	5th	Green	At Least 300 Times
Chung-Gun	4th	Blue	At Least 300 Times
Toi-Gye	3rd	Blue	At Least 300 Times
Hwa-Rang	2nd	Brown	At Least 300 Times
Chung-Mu	1st	Brown	At Least 300 Times

REQUIREMENTS FOR
1ST DEGREE BLACK BELT

1. Right attitude and good character.

2. Mastery of the aforementioned nine patterns.

3. Capability of breaking three, one-inch pine boards with the following techniques:

   a. straight punch

   b. knife hand strike

   c. front or roundhouse kick

   d. side snap kick

4. Good free-sparring ability coupled with well-controlled techniques.

5. Ability and willingness to teach the tenets of Tae Kwon Do to others.

TAN-GUN HYUNG

Tan-Gun Hyung: The second pattern of the Chang-Hon School, which contains 21 movements, is named after a legendary Korean hero who reputedly founded Korea in 2334 B.C.

DIAGRAM

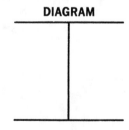

TAN-GUN AT A GLANCE

READY   1   2

7   8   9   10

15   16   17   18

SIDE VIEW

BACK VIEW

OTHER VIEW

STEP DIAGRAM

FRONT VIEW

CHUNBI SOGI
(Ready Stance)

Assume a parallel ready stance.

NOTE: All pivotal turns indicated in degrees, either clockwise or counterclockwise, refer to the directional turn of the face. Star symbols (★) indicate KIHAP (yelling).

TOP VIEW	APPLICATION

BEGINNING FRONT VIEW

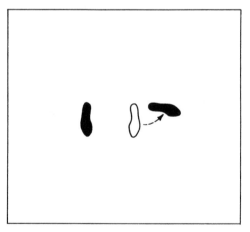

INTERMEDIATE FRONT VIEW

OTHER VIEW

STEP DIAGRAM

22

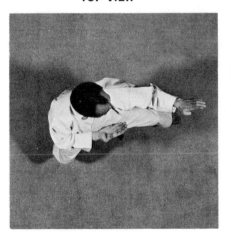

FINAL FRONT VIEW

1. CHUNGDAN SUDO MARKI
(Middle Knife Hand)

Pivot on the right foot 90 degrees counter-clockwise, assuming a right back stance as you execute a middle guarding block with the left knife hand.★

TOP VIEW   **APPLICATION**

23

BEGINNING FRONT VIEW

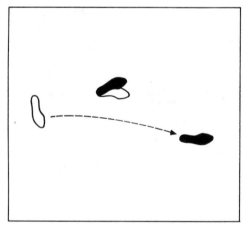

INTERMEDIATE FRONT VIEW

OTHER VIEW

STEP DIAGRAM

24

2. SANGDAN CHIRUGI
(High Punch)

Take a straight step with the right foot, assuming a right front stance as you execute a high punch with the right fist.

FINAL FRONT VIEW

TOP VIEW   **APPLICATION**

BEGINNING FRONT VIEW **INTERMEDIATE FRONT VIEW**

OTHER VIEW **STEP DIAGRAM**

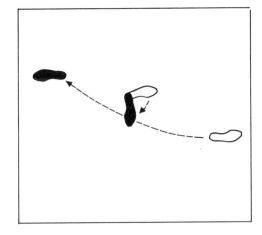

3. CHUNGDAN SUDO MARKI
(Middle Knife Hand Block)

Pivot on the left foot 180 degrees clockwise, assuming a left back stance as you execute a middle guarding block with the right knife hand.

FINAL FRONT VIEW

TOP VIEW

APPLICATION

BEGINNING FRONT VIEW

INTERMEDIATE FRONT VIEW

OTHER VIEW

STEP DIAGRAM

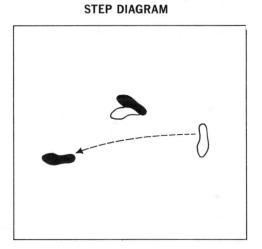

FINAL FRONT VIEW

4. SANGDAN CHIRUGI
(High Punch)

Take a straight step with the left foot, assuming a left front stance as you execute a high punch with the left fist.

| **TOP VIEW** | **APPLICATION** |

29

BEGINNING FRONT VIEW

INTERMEDIATE FRONT VIEW

OTHER VIEW

STEP DIAGRAM

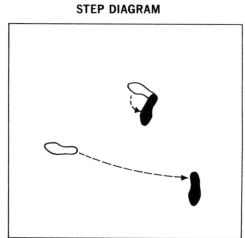

30

5. HARDAN PALMOK MARKI
(Low Forearm Block)

Pivot on the right foot 90 degrees counterclockwise, assuming a left front stance while you execute a low block with the left forearm.

FINAL FRONT VIEW

TOP VIEW

APPLICATION

BEGINNING FRONT VIEW   **INTERMEDIATE FRONT VIEW**

OTHER VIEW   **STEP DIAGRAM**

 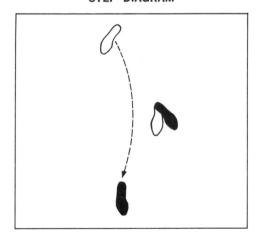

32

6. SANGDAN CHIRUGI
(High Punch)

Take a straight step with the right foot as you execute a high punch with the right fist.

FINAL FRONT VIEW

TOP VIEW

APPLICATION

BEGINNING FRONT VIEW

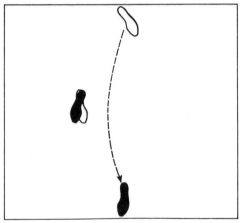

INTERMEDIATE FRONT VIEW

OTHER VIEW

STEP DIAGRAM

FINAL FRONT VIEW

7. SANGDAN CHIRUGI
(High Punch)

Take a straight step with the left foot, assuming a left front stance as you execute a high punch with the left fist.

TOP VIEW	APPLICATION

BEGINNING FRONT VIEW

INTERMEDIATE FRONT VIEW

OTHER VIEW

STEP DIAGRAM

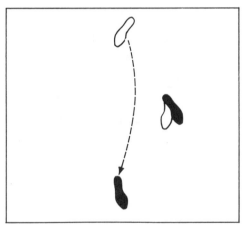

FINAL FRONT VIEW

8. SANGDAN CHIRUGI
(High Punch)

Take a straight step with the right foot as you execute a high, right-fist punch. ★

TOP VIEW

APPLICATION

BEGINNING FRONT VIEW   **INTERMEDIATE FRONT VIEW**

OTHER VIEW   **STEP DIAGRAM**

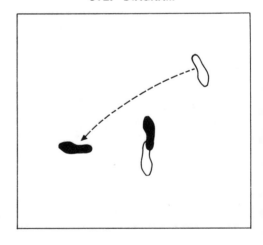

FINAL FRONT VIEW

9. SANG PALMOK MARKI
(Twin Forearm Block)

Pivot on the right foot 270 degrees counter-clockwise, assuming a right back stance as you execute a twin forearm block.

TOP VIEW   **APPLICATION**

BEGINNING FRONT VIEW

INTERMEDIATE FRONT VIEW

OTHER VIEW

STEP DIAGRAM

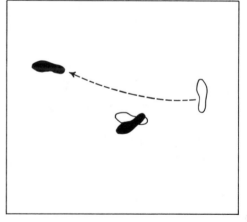

FINAL FRONT VIEW

10. SANGDAN CHIRUGI
(High Punch)

Take a straight step with the right foot, assuming a right front stance as you execute a high punch with the right fist.

TOP VIEW	APPLICATION

BEGINNING FRONT VIEW

INTERMEDIATE FRONT VIEW

OTHER VIEW

STEP DIAGRAM

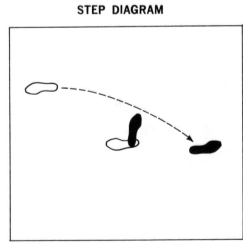

42

FINAL FRONT VIEW

11. SSANG PALMOK MARKI
(Twin Forearm Block)

Pivot on the left foot 180 degrees clockwise, assuming a left back stance as you execute a twin forearm block.

TOP VIEW	APPLICATION

43

BEGINNING FRONT VIEW   **INTERMEDIATE FRONT VIEW**

OTHER VIEW   **STEP DIAGRAM**

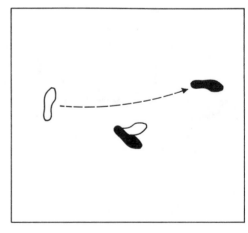

12. SANGDAN CHIRUGI
(High Punch)

Take a straight step with the left foot, assuming a left front stance as you execute a high punch with the left fist.

FINAL FRONT VIEW

TOP VIEW	**APPLICATION**

BEGINNING FRONT VIEW

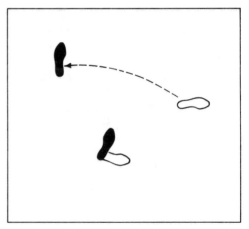

INTERMEDIATE FRONT VIEW

OTHER VIEW

STEP DIAGRAM

46

FINAL FRONT VIEW

13. HARDAN PALMOK MARKI
(Low Forearm Block)

Pivot on the right foot 90 degrees counter-clockwise, assuming a left front stance as you execute a low block with the left forearm.

TOP VIEW	APPLICATION

47

BEGINNING FRONT VIEW   **INTERMEDIATE FRONT VIEW**

OTHER VIEW   **STEP DIAGRAM**

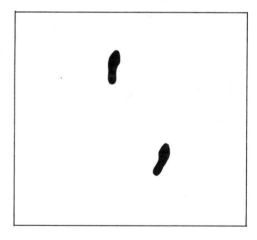

14. CHUKYO MARKI
(Rising Block)

Without pausing or changing stance, execute a rising block with the left forearm. (13 and 14 are done in fast combination.)

FINAL FRONT VIEW

TOP VIEW

APPLICATION

BEGINNING FRONT VIEW **INTERMEDIATE FRONT VIEW**

OTHER VIEW **STEP DIAGRAM**

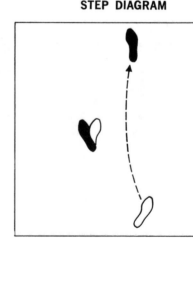

15. CHUKYO MARKI
(Rising Block)

Take a straight step with the right foot, assuming a right front stance as you execute a rising block with the right forearm.

FINAL FRONT VIEW

TOP VIEW

APPLICATION

BEGINNING FRONT VIEW   **INTERMEDIATE FRONT VIEW**

OTHER VIEW   **STEP DIAGRAM**

 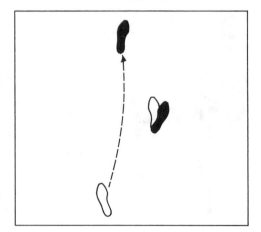

16. CHUKYO MARKI
(Rising Block)

Take a straight step with the left foot, assuming a left front stance as you execute a rising block with the left forearm.

FINAL FRONT VIEW

TOP VIEW	APPLICATION

BEGINNING FRONT VIEW

INTERMEDIATE FRONT VIEW

OTHER VIEW

STEP DIAGRAM

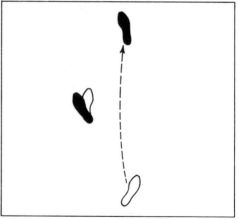

17. CHUKYO MARKI

(Rising Block)

Take a straight step with the right foot, assuming a right front stance as you execute a rising block with the right forearm.

FINAL FRONT VIEW

| **TOP VIEW** | **APPLICATION** |

BEGINNING FRONT VIEW

INTERMEDIATE FRONT VIEW

OTHER VIEW

STEP DIAGRAM

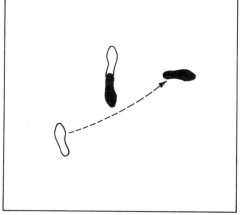

18. CHUNGDAN SUDO YOP TAERIGI
(Middle Knife Hand Side Strike)

Pivot on the right foot 270 degrees counterclockwise, assuming a right back stance as you execute a middle strike with the left knife hand.

FINAL FRONT VIEW

TOP VIEW

APPLICATION

BEGINNING FRONT VIEW   **INTERMEDIATE FRONT VIEW**

OTHER VIEW   **STEP DIAGRAM**

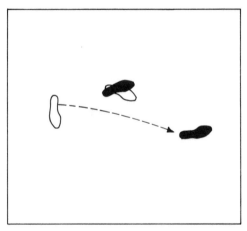

FINAL FRONT VIEW

19. SANGDAN CHIRUGI
(High Punch)

Take a straight step with the right foot, assuming a right front stance as you execute a high punch with the right fist.

TOP VIEW	APPLICATION

BEGINNING FRONT VIEW

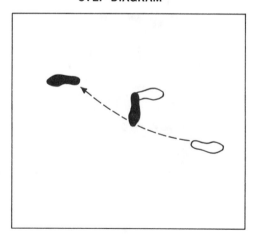

INTERMEDIATE FRONT VIEW

OTHER VIEW

STEP DIAGRAM

20. CHUNGDAN SUDO YOP TAERIGI
(Middle Knife Hand Side Strike)

Pivot on the left foot 180 degrees clockwise, assuming a left back stance as you execute a middle strike with the right knife hand.

FINAL FRONT VIEW

TOP VIEW

APPLICATION

BEGINNING FRONT VIEW

INTERMEDIATE FRONT VIEW

OTHER VIEW

STEP DIAGRAM

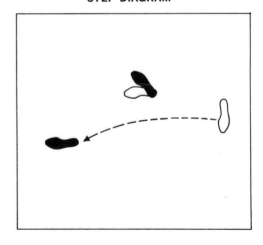

21. SANGDAN CHIRUGI
(High Punch)

Take a straight step with the left foot, assuming a left front stance as you execute a high punch with the left fist. ✱

FINAL FRONT VIEW

TOP VIEW

APPLICATION

SIDE VIEW

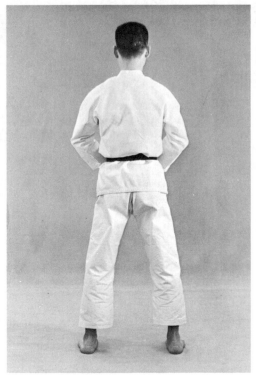

BACK VIEW

OTHER VIEW

STEP DIAGRAM

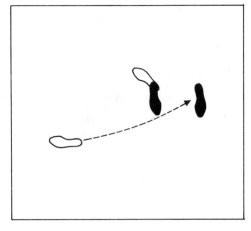

FRONT VIEW

GOMAN
(End)

Bring the left foot backward, assuming a parallel ready stance.

TOP VIEW	APPLICATION

TO-SAN HYUNG

To-San Hyung: The name of this pattern commemorates the pseudonym of a great Korean patriot and educator Ahn Ch'ang Ho (1876-1938). This pattern contains 24 movements.

DIAGRAM

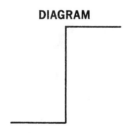

TO-SAN AT A GLANCE

READY

| 5 | 6 | 7 |

| 12 | 13 | 14 |

| 19 | 20 | 21 |

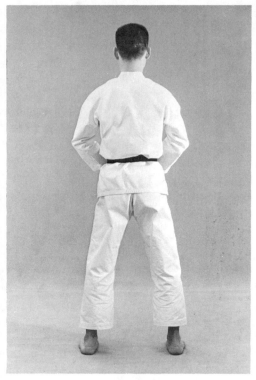

SIDE VIEW

BACK VIEW

OTHER VIEW

STEP DIAGRAM

CHUNBI SOGI
(Ready Stance)

Assume a parallel ready stance.

NOTE: All pivotal turns indicated in degrees, either clockwise or counterclockwise, refer to the directional turn of the face. Star symbols (★) indicate KIHAP (yelling).

FRONT VIEW

TOP VIEW

APPLICATION

71

BEGINNING FRONT VIEW

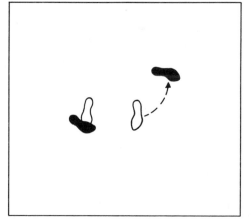

INTERMEDIATE FRONT VIEW

OTHER VIEW

STEP DIAGRAM

1. SANGDAN PALMOK MARKI
(High Forearm Block)

Pivot on the right foot 90 degrees counter-clockwise, assuming a left front stance as you execute a high block with the left forearm.★

FINAL FRONT VIEW

TOP VIEW

APPLICATION

73

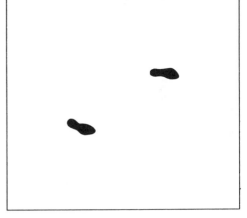

OTHER VIEW

STEP DIAGRAM

2. CHUNGDAN PANDAE CHIRUGI
(Middle Reverse Punch)

Execute a middle reverse punch with the right fist.

FINAL FRONT VIEW

TOP VIEW

APPLICATION

BEGINNING FRONT VIEW

INTERMEDIATE FRONT VIEW

OTHER VIEW

STEP DIAGRAM

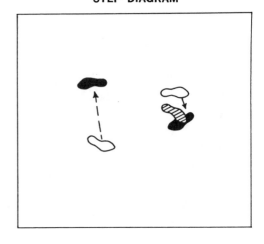

FINAL FRONT VIEW

3. SANGDAN PALMOK MARKI
(High Forearm Block)

Move the left foot about one-half shoulder width to the right and pivot on it 180 degrees clockwise, assuming a right front stance as you execute a high block with the right forearm.

TOP VIEW

APPLICATION

OTHER VIEW

STEP DIAGRAM

 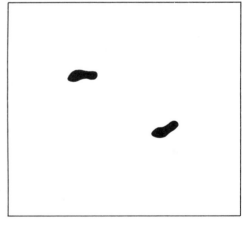

4. CHUNGDAN PANDAE CHIRUGI
(Middle Reverse Punch)

Execute a middle reverse punch with the left fist.

FINAL FRONT VIEW

TOP VIEW	APPLICATION

BEGINNING FRONT VIEW　　　　**INTERMEDIATE FRONT VIEW**

OTHER VIEW　　　　**STEP DIAGRAM**

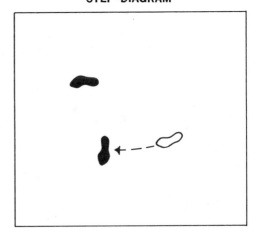

5. CHUNGDAN SUDO MARKI
(Middle Knife Hand Block)

Pivot on the right foot 90 degrees counter-clockwise, assuming a right back stance as you execute a middle guarding block with the left knife hand.

FINAL FRONT VIEW

TOP VIEW	APPLICATION

BEGINNING FRONT VIEW

INTERMEDIATE FRONT VIEW

OTHER VIEW

STEP DIAGRAM

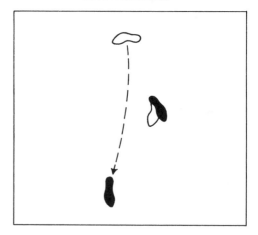

FINAL FRONT VIEW

6. CHUNGDAN KWANSU
(Middle Spear Finger)

Take a straight step with the right foot, assuming a right front stance as you execute a vertical spear finger thrust with the right hand. ★

TOP VIEW	**APPLICATION**

BEGINNING FRONT VIEW

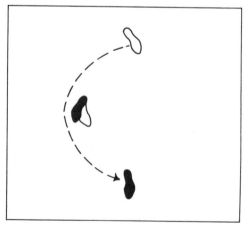

INTERMEDIATE FRONT VIEW

OTHER VIEW

STEP DIAGRAM

FINAL FRONT VIEW

7. SANGDAN YIKWON TAERIGI
(High Back Fist Strike)

Pivot on the right foot 360 degrees counter-clockwise, assuming a left front stance as you execute a high side strike with the left back fist.

TOP VIEW	APPLICATION

BEGINNING FRONT VIEW

INTERMEDIATE FRONT VIEW

OTHER VIEW

STEP DIAGRAM

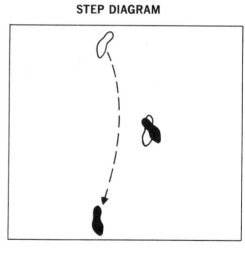

FINAL FRONT VIEW

8. SANGDAN YIKWON TAERIGI
(High Back Fist Strike)

Take a straight step with the right foot, assuming a right front stance as you execute a high side strike with the right back fist.

TOP VIEW	APPLICATION

BEGINNING FRONT VIEW

INTERMEDIATE FRONT VIEW

OTHER VIEW

STEP DIAGRAM

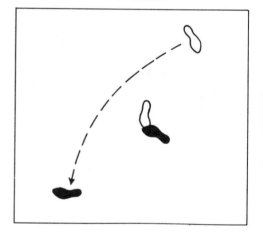

FINAL FRONT VIEW

9. SANGDAN PALMOK MARKI
(High Forearm Block)

Pivot on the right foot 270 degrees counter-clockwise, assuming a left front stance as you execute a high block with the left forearm.

TOP VIEW

APPLICATION

BEGINNING FRONT VIEW

INTERMEDIATE FRONT VIEW

OTHER VIEW

STEP DIAGRAM

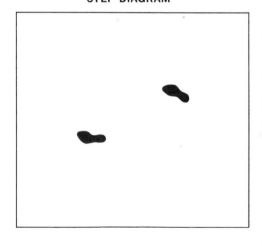

10. CHUNGDAN PANDAE CHIRUGI
(Middle Reverse Punch)

Execute a middle reverse punch with the right fist.

FINAL FRONT VIEW

TOP VIEW	APPLICATION

BEGINNING FRONT VIEW   **INTERMEDIATE FRONT VIEW**

OTHER VIEW   **STEP DIAGRAM**

11. PALMOK SANGDAN MARKI
(Forearm High Block)

Move the left foot about one-half shoulder width to the right and pivot on it 180 degrees clockwise as you execute a high block with the right forearm.

FINAL FRONT VIEW

TOP VIEW	**APPLICATION**

OTHER VIEW

STEP DIAGRAM

FINAL FRONT VIEW

12. CHUNGDAN PANDAE CHIRUGI
(Middle Reverse Punch)

Execute a middle reverse punch with the left fist.

TOP VIEW

APPLICATION

BEGINNING FRONT VIEW

INTERMEDIATE FRONT VIEW

OTHER VIEW

STEP DIAGRAM

96

13. PALMOK HAECHO MARKI
(Forearm Spreading Block)

Pivot on the right foot 135 degrees counter-clockwise, assuming a left front stance as you execute a high-spreading block with both forearms.

FINAL FRONT VIEW

| **TOP VIEW** | **APPLICATION** |

97

OTHER VIEW

STEP DIAGRAM

 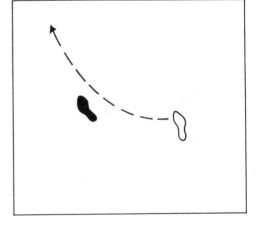

FINAL FRONT VIEW

14. CHUNGDAN AP CHAGI
(Middle Front Snap Kick)

Execute a middle front snap kick with the right leg without changing hand positions.

TOP VIEW

APPLICATION

BEGINNING FRONT VIEW

INTERMEDIATE FRONT VIEW

OTHER VIEW

STEP DIAGRAM

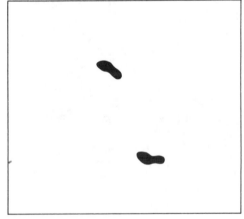

15. CHUNGDAN CHIRUGI

(Middle Punch)

Take a straight step with the kicking foot, assuming a right front stance as you execute a middle punch with the right fist.

FINAL FRONT VIEW

TOP VIEW

APPLICATION

STEP DIAGRAM

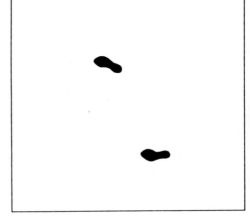

FINAL FRONT VIEW

16. CHUNGDAN PANDAE CHIRUGI

(Middle Reverse Punch)

Execute a middle punch with the left fist. (14, 15 and 16 are done in fast combination.)

TOP VIEW	APPLICATION

BEGINNING FRONT VIEW

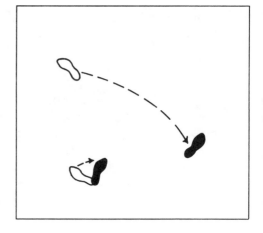

INTERMEDIATE FRONT VIEW

OTHER VIEW

STEP DIAGRAM

104

17. PALMOK HAECHO MARKI
(Forearm Spreading Block)

Pivot on the left foot 90 degrees clockwise, assuming a right front stance as you execute a high-spreading block with both forearms.

FINAL FRONT VIEW

TOP VIEW

APPLICATION

BEGINNING FRONT VIEW   **INTERMEDIATE FRONT VIEW**

OTHER VIEW   STEP DIAGRAM

 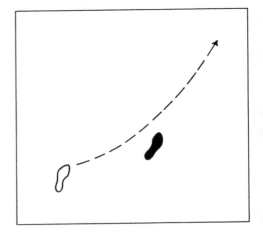

FINAL FRONT VIEW

18. CHUNGDAN AP CHAGI
(Middle Front Snap Kick)

Execute a middle front snap kick with the left foot without changing hand positions.

TOP VIEW	APPLICATION

BEGINNING FRONT VIEW

INTERMEDIATE FRONT VIEW

OTHER VIEW

STEP DIAGRAM

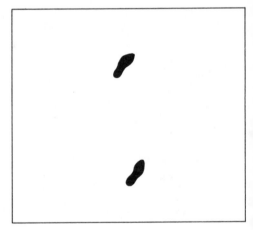

19. CHUNGDAN CHIRUGI
(Middle Punch)

Take a straight step with the kicking foot, assuming a left front stance as you execute a middle punch with the left fist.

FINAL FRONT VIEW

TOP VIEW

APPLICATION

OTHER VIEW

STEP DIAGRAM

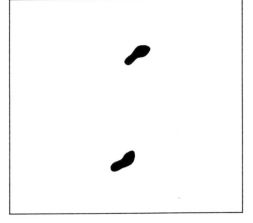

FINAL FRONT VIEW

20. CHUNGDAN PANDAE CHIRUGI
(Middle Reverse Punch)

Execute a middle punch with the right fist.
(18, 19 and 20 are done in fast combination.)

TOP VIEW	APPLICATION

BEGINNING FRONT VIEW

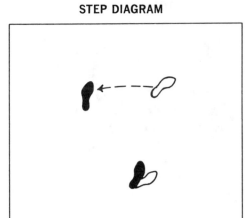

INTERMEDIATE FRONT VIEW

OTHER VIEW

STEP DIAGRAM

21. CHUKYO MARKI
(Rising Block)

Pivot on the right foot 45 degrees counter-clockwise, assuming a left front stance as you execute a rising block with the left forearm.

FINAL FRONT VIEW

TOP VIEW

APPLICATION

BEGINNING FRONT VIEW

INTERMEDIATE FRONT VIEW

OTHER VIEW

STEP DIAGRAM

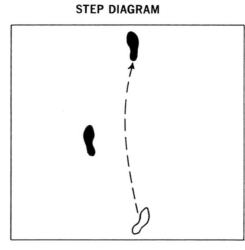

22. CHUKYO MARKI
(Rising Block)

Take a straight step with the right foot, assuming a right front stance as you execute a rising block with the right forearm.

FINAL FRONT VIEW

TOP VIEW	APPLICATION

BEGINNING FRONT VIEW

INTERMEDIATE FRONT VIEW

OTHER VIEW

STEP DIAGRAM

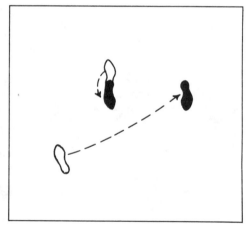

23. CHUNGDAN SUDO YOP TAERIGI
(Middle Knife Hand Side Strike)

Pivot on the right foot 270 degrees counter-clockwise, assuming a riding stance as you execute a middle side strike with the left knife hand.

FINAL FRONT VIEW

TOP VIEW

APPLICATION

117

BEGINNING FRONT VIEW

INTERMEDIATE FRONT VIEW

OTHER VIEW

STEP DIAGRAM

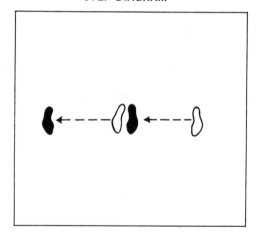

24. CHUNGDAN SUDO YOP TAERIGI
(Middle Knife Hand Side Strike)

Bring the left foot alongside the right foot and then take a side step with the right foot, assuming a riding stance as you execute a middle side strike with the knife hand.★

FINAL FRONT VIEW

TOP VIEW

APPLICATION

119

SIDE VIEW

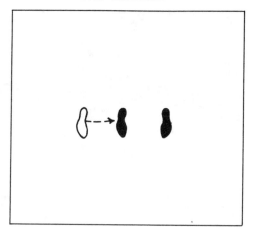

BACK VIEW

OTHER VIEW

STEP DIAGRAM

GOMAN
(End)

Bring the right foot toward the left, assuming a parallel ready stance.

FRONT VIEW

| **TOP VIEW** | **APPLICATION** |

COMBINATION ATTACK TECHNIQUES

The practice of combination techniques naturally follows the learning of basics. Although the objective of Tae Kwon Do is to overcome an opponent with individual techniques as learned in one-step sparring, it is important that the student prepare himself for any situation. Practice of combination techniques is the second stepping stone to free sparring. After diligently and correctly practicing these techniques you will have begun development of the balance, coordination and ability necessary to deliver a multiple attack consisting of several individual techniques. This ability is extremely important in free sparring against a person who is also trained, as he will possibly have the ability to block your initial blow. In addition, you will be prepared for self-defense against more than one attacker.

Practice each combination until it feels natural and you maintain balance and control over your body. Practice with maximum power, and always imagine a target for each blow in the combination technique.

1   2   3

FREE-STYLE REVERSE PUNCH

(1) Assume a free-sparring stance. Avoid telegraphing the punch by holding your back fist motionless prior to the execution of the punch. (2) Twist your lower hip about 90 degrees in order to apply all your body weight to the punch. Keep your head in the same direction so that you can watch your opponent. With your toes pointing forward, execute the punch by pivoting on the ball of the rear foot and lifting your heel up in order to give your hip freedom to twist. Bring your other fist up to guard your face, and your elbow to guard your mid-section. (3) Return to original position.

SIDE VIEW

APPLICATION

1

2

ROUNDHOUSE KICK

(1) Assume a free-sparring stance. (2) Keep your body as erect as possible as you cock your knee up high. (3) Turn your hip about 90 degrees in order to apply your body weight to the kick. Keep the heel of the supporting foot on the ground for stability. (4) Bring your foot back quickly and keep your balance. (5) Return to the original position.

3

5

4

125

FRONT KICK — REVERSE PUNCH

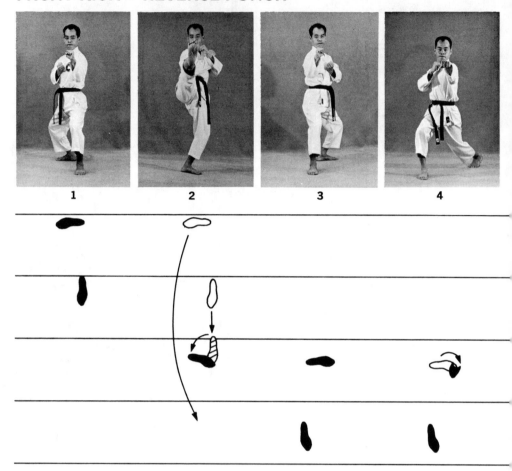

(1) Assume a right-hand, free-sparring stance. (2) Hop and slide one step forward and deliver front kick. (3) Drop your right foot and assume a left-hand, free-sparring stance. (4) Lift the heel of your rear foot so that your hip can be easily twisted for the reverse punch. (5) End in a left-hand, free-sparring stance.

5

APPLICATION

ROUNDHOUSE KICK — REVERSE PUNCH

1   2   3   4

(1) Assume a left-hand, free-sparring stance. (2) Deliver rear-foot round-house kick. (3) Keep your body as erect as possible in order to follow through with the next technique. (4) If your body is leaning backward, it will be diffi-cult to straighten up and attack with the reverse punch. (5) As you deliver the reverse punch, make sure the rear heel is lifted up high so that your hip can be twisted quickly, but comfortably. (6) End in a right-hand, free-spar-ring stance.

5   6

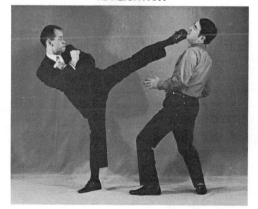

APPLICATION

FRONT KICK – ROUNDHOUSE KICK – REVERSE PUNCH

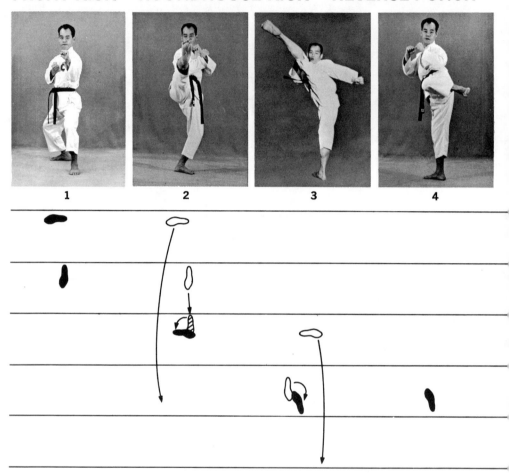

1   2   3   4

APPLICATION

(1) Assume a right-hand, free-sparring stance. (2) Slide one step forward, immediately delivering the rear-foot (right foot, in this case) front kick without delay. (3) As your right foot lands, follow up immediately with the left-foot roundhouse kick, keeping your body as erect as possible. (4) Drop your left foot to the floor. (5) Prepare to deliver reverse punch. (6) Deliver reverse punch. (7) End in a right-hand, free-sparring stance.

5   6   7

ROUNDHOUSE KICK — SIDE KICK

1   2   3   4

(1) Assume a right-hand, free-sparring stance. (2) Deliver rear-foot (right foot) roundhouse kick. (3) Drop your right foot to the floor. (4) Cross your left foot behind your right foot as quickly as possible, as in a skip. (5) Begin side kick. (6) Complete side kick. (7) End in a left-hand, free-sparring stance.

5   6   7

APPLICATION

RIGHT AND LEFT FOOT ROUNDHOUSE KICKS — REVERSE

1   2   3   4

APPLICATION

(1) Assume a right-hand, free-sparring stance. (2) Deliver rear-foot (right foot) roundhouse kick. (3) Return right foot to the floor, keeping your body as erect as possible. (4) Deliver left-foot round-house kick. (5) Return left foot to the floor. (6) Prepare to deliver reverse punch. (7) Deliver reverse punch. (8) Return to a right-hand, free-sparring stance.

5   6   7   8

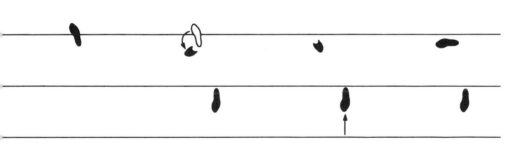

ONE-TWO PUNCH — SIDE KICK

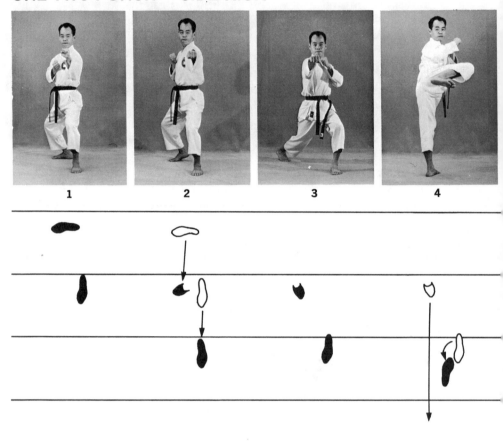

1   2   3   4

APPLICATION

(1) Assume a right-hand, free-sparring stance. (2) Step-slide forward and deliver left-hand front punch. (3) Deliver reverse punch. (4) Begin delivery of side kick. (5) Complete side kick. (6) End in a left-hand, free-sparring stance.

5   6

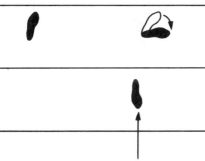

ROUNDHOUSE KICK — BACK TURN SIDE KICK — REVERSE

1 2 3 4

APPLICATION

(1) Assume a right-hand, free-sparring stance. (2) Deliver rear-foot (right foot) roundhouse kick. (3) Return right foot to the floor with the heel pointing toward the opponent so that you can (4) & (5) immediately perform the back turn side kick without losing your balance. (6) Prepare to deliver reverse punch. (7) Deliver reverse punch. (8) Return to right-hand, free-sparring stance.

5   6   7   8

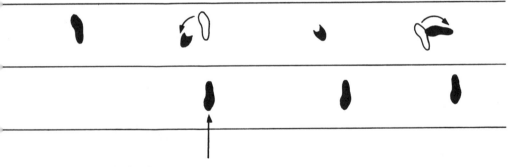

ROUNDHOUSE KICK — REVERSE PUNCH — ROUNDHOUSE

1 2 3 4

(1) Assume a right-hand, free-sparring stance. (2) Deliver rear-foot (right foot) roundhouse kick. (3) Return right foot to the floor and simultaneously execute reverse punch. (4) Bring left foot forward to right foot and twist your hips 90 degrees in order to give momentum when coming back for the second roundhouse kick. (5) Deliver second, rear-foot (right foot) roundhouse kick. (6) Return right foot to the floor. (7) End in a left-hand, free-sparring stance.

5

6

7

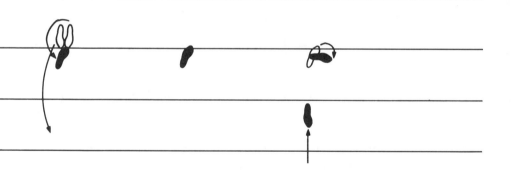

BACK SIDE KICK — ROUNDHOUSE KICK — REVERSE PUNCH

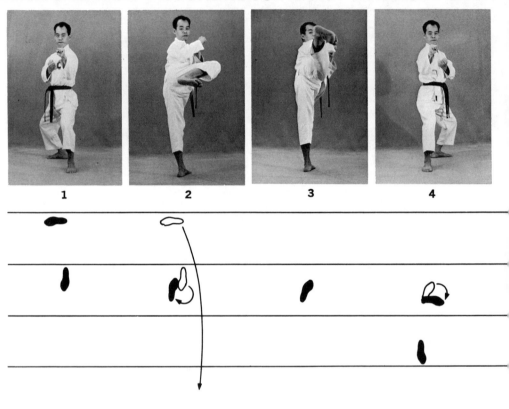

| 1 | 2 | 3 | 4 |

APPLICATION

(1) Assume a right-hand, free-sparring stance. (2) Keeping your body erect, turn clockwise and lift your right knee as high as possible. (3) Deliver rear-foot (right foot), back side kick. (4) Return right foot to the floor. (5) Deliver left-foot roundhouse kick. (6) Return left foot to the floor and prepare to deliver reverse punch. (7) Deliver reverse punch. (8) End in a right-hand, free-sparring stance.

5   6   7   8

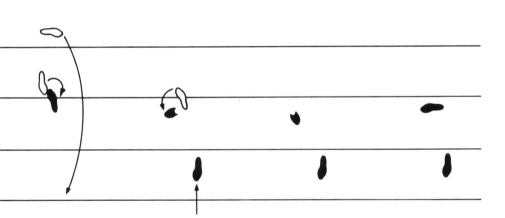

REVERSE PUNCH — ROUNDHOUSE KICK

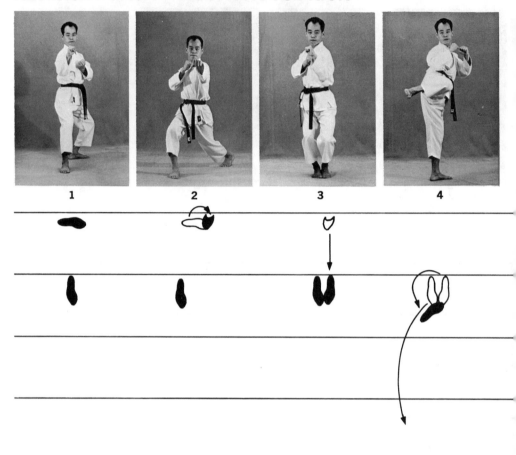

(1) Assume a left-hand, free-sparring stance. (2) Begin execution of the reverse punch. (3) Bring left foot forward to right foot and twist your hips 90 degrees in order to give momentum in executing the (4) & (5) front-foot (right foot) roundhouse kick. (6) Return right foot to the floor. (7) Return to a left-hand, free-sparring stance.

5   6   7

APPLICATION

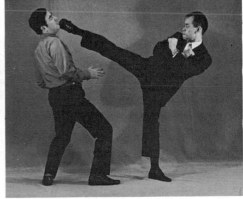

FRONT BACK FIST — SIDE KICK — REVERSE PUNCH

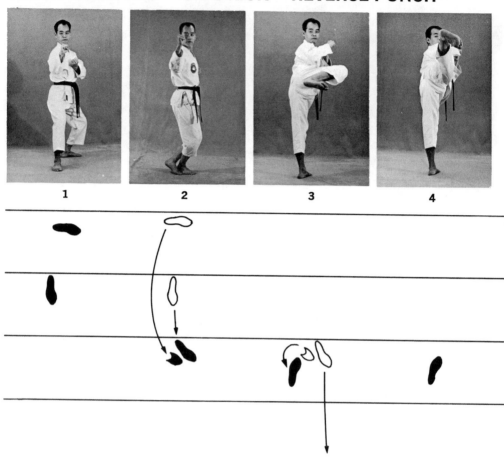

1   2   3   4

APPLICATION

(1) Assume a left-hand, free-sparring stance. (2) Hop forward, crossing the left foot behind the right foot and simultaneously delivering a back fist to the face area of the opponent in order to make him block high. His midsection should now be open for attack. Immediately follow with (3) & (4) skip side kick. (5) Return right root to the floor. (6) Prepare to deliver reverse punch. (7) Deliver reverse punch.

5   6   7

REVERSE STANCE — SIDE KICK — REVERSE PUNCH

1 2 3 4

(1) Assume a right-hand, free-sparring stance. (2) Quickly reverse to a left-hand, free-sparring stance. (3) Skip forward, crossing your left foot behind your right foot. Note: Steps 1, 2 and 3 must be performed as quickly as possible in order to capitalize on the element of surprise. (4) and (5) Deliver side kick. (6) Return right foot to the floor. (7) Prepare to deliver reverse punch. (8) Deliver reverse punch.

5   **6**   **7**   **8**

APPLICATION

BASIC SELF-DEFENSE TECHNIQUES

One of the many benefits received from Tae Kwon Do training is the ability to defend against attack, whether the attacker has the advantage of size, strength or weapon. On the following pages you will find defenses against many of the more common attacks by an opponent. Later we shall cover defenses against multiple attack and attack with a weapon.

Each of the techniques shown should be practiced with another person until you become proficient and the technique is almost a reflex action. Practice each technique as illustrated and then reverse the attack and practice defending with the opposite hand and foot.

Although an effort has been made to show you all the most common grabbing attacks, it is doubtful that you would be attacked exactly as illustrated and under the same conditions. For this reason, it is important that you understand the principles involved in each defense so you will be able to react quickly and properly to an unusual attack and use good Tae Kwon Do techniques, even though you may not have practiced for that specific attack. As you practice, analyze what each move is doing for you. Practice slowly at first and gradually build up speed as you understand the principle. After you have become proficient against the attacks shown, practice applying your defense techniques against new situations by having your partner attack or grab you in any manner.

The practicing of these self-defense techniques is enjoyable because you will see the practical application of much of your basic training. But remember, practice seriously and diligently as if your life depended on each move. You may never be confronted with a real situation on the street or elsewhere. But if you are, the difference could be in how well you are prepared.

When attacked from the back . . .

lift your left arm up straight, stepping back and across, with your left foot outside the attacker's right foot.

Pivot your foot so that the toes of both feet are pointing at your attacker. Lock your arm over and around both of his arms with your left arm.

Lift your right knee sharply up and forward to the groin.

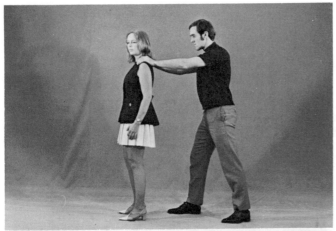

When attacked from the back you can also . . .

cross your left arm high over the right as illustrated. The hands should be held tensed as in a sudo or chop.

Step back slightly with your left foot to a point directly in front and between the feet of your attacker. At the same time bring your left arm around quickly, fully extending and delivering the blow with the outside of the hand to the attacker's neck. To develop more force, immediately pull your right hand back to the right side of your waist, a maneuver which also prepares you for the delivery of an additional punch if necessary.

When your right arm is grabbed by an attacker's left hand . . .

turn your right arm to the inside so your hand is palm up. Cover the attacker's hand with your left hand.

Pull attacker's hand toward you and push your elbow toward him to loosen his grip.

Grab the base of his thumb with your right hand and squeeze his hand between yours.

In a clockwise movement twist attacker's arm outward and away from his body.

When grabbed by the wrist . . .

step back with the left foot, bending the front leg slightly. Your feet should be approximately shoulders' width apart for balance.

Note that the stance assumed is that of the Chongul or front stance.

From the front stance position bring the left leg forward and up, sharply delivering a front kick with the toe of the foot (shoe) to the groin area.

When your right hand is grabbed by an attacker's right hand . . .

cover the back of the attacker's hand with your left hand. Press your middle finger firmly into the muscle between the attacker's thumb and index finger.

Lift your right arm so it is erect and push forward, bending attacker's arm.

Bring your right hand down on top of attacker's arm and press down hard.

157

When grabbed by the arm from the opposite side . . .

pivot, assuming a Fugul or basic back stance, so that the side of your body is facing your attacker.

Lift your front leg (the one closest to the attacker) as high as possible, bending at the knee.

While pulling the arm of your attacker and pivoting, thrust and lock your leg as in a side kick. The blow should be delivered forcibly with the heel of your shoe and directed toward the attacker's midsection.

When your purse is grabbed from the front...

Remember: When carrying a purse, the first defense is to always have a secure grasp on the strap.

step back with the foot opposite the purse, bending the front leg slightly (Chongul or front stance).

Bring the back foot up and through sharply, locking the knee and driving the toe of your foot (shoe) into the groin.

Immediately bend the knee of the same leg and bring it up sharply to the midsection or face of the attacker.

In the event that someone from behind runs past, grabs your purse and tries to escape . . .

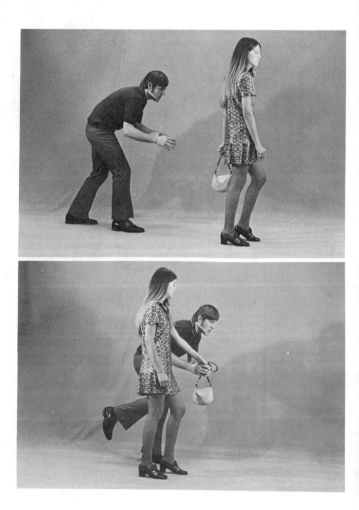

keep a tight grip on the purse.

Pull the purse toward you and at the same time bring your foot on the opposite side up and around, locking the leg out straight and driving the toe of your foot (shoe) into the midsection of the attacker.

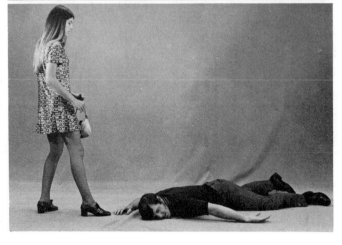

You are now in a position to run for help or deliver another kick to the attacker if necessary.

When grabbed from behind with your arms locked down . . .

step directly to the left, bending your knees and squatting down. At the same time quickly snap both arms straight forward.

Bring your right arm back, driving your elbow into the midsection or solar plexis of your attacker.

Immediately turn your arm so that your fist is upward.

Thrust upward with a punch to the jaw.

When attacked from behind you can also . . .

step directly to the left, bending your knees and squatting down (horseback stance). At the same time quickly snap both arms straight forward.

Bring the right elbow back sharply to the groin or pelvic area.

164

As the attacker doubles over, bring your right arm around his side and lock up over his left arm.

Twist your body to the left, throwing your hip into the attacker's midsection in order to throw him over your hip and to the ground.

From this point you are free to run for safety or deliver an additional kick to the head if necessary.

165

When you are grabbed by both wrists . . .

open your left hand and grab the attacker's left wrist as you snap your right wrist out of his hold.

Continue around with your right arm so your elbow is back.

Bring the elbow back sharply, driving into the attacker's midsection.

When grabbed by both wrists from the front you can also . . .

lift both your arms outward and upward.

Step forward toward your attacker with your left foot just in front of his right foot.

Bring your right leg forward and upward, sharply driving your knee into the groin.

When attacked from the front with a bear hug . . .

step back with the right foot and bend the front knee. At the same time grab the top of both of your attacker's arms with your hands.

Bring the rear foot up and through sharply driving the knee to the groin.

As your attacker begins to double over, pivot around to your right and lock your left arm over your attacker's arm.

Again, bring the right knee up and through, and deliver the knee kick to your attacker's face.

When grabbed with a bear hug from the front you can also . . .

step back with the right foot, bending the left knee slightly and at the same time allowing your body to drop straight down. Bring your right arm back with your palm up and the tips of the fingers slightly curled and tensed.

Thrust the right arm up and forward between the attacker's arms, and drive the palm of your hand up and under the chin.

Bring the back leg up and forward, driving the knee into the groin.

170

When grabbed by the shoulders or neck from the front...

step back with the right foot, bending the front leg slightly and pulling the right arm back—palm up and tensed. Fingers should be slightly bent but held very firm.

Thrust your right hand up and forward between the arms of your attacker and drive your first two fingers into his eyes. At the same time draw your left arm back to your waist with your fist clenched tight.

Thrust your left arm forward, driving your fist into the throat of your attacker, and at the same time pull your right arm back to your waist with your fist clenched.

**When attacked
from the front
at the shoulders
or throat
you can also . . .**

step back with the right foot,
slightly bending the front leg.

Cross your wrists directly in
front of your solar plexis with
the palms facing yourself.

Thrusting both arms upward and outward and, at the same time, turning your palms outward, hit your attacker's arms as close to his wrists as possible.

Bring the palms of both hands sharply to your attacker's ears.

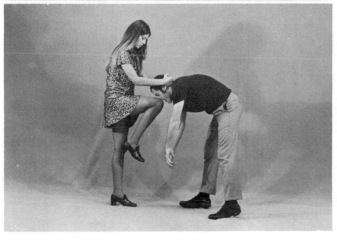

Grab the back of your attacker's head or his hair. Bring your right knee up sharply and at the same time pull his head down, delivering the blow to his face.

When your shoulder is grabbed by an attacker using his arm on the same side . . .

grab the attacker's hand firmly on top with your opposite hand and twist it counterclockwise so his little finger is up and his thumb is down.

Lift your other arm (the side the attacker's hand is on) up high.

Bring this arm over and down around the attacker's wrist so that his wrist is deep in your armpit. Tighten up.

Put pressure downward on his wrist by applying your whole body weight. Be sure to keep his hand in such a position that his little finger is up and his thumb down.

When your head
is locked and
you are in
danger of being
punched . . .

grab the attacker's right arm
with your left hand.

Bring your right arm behind, up
and over his left shoulder and
put your little finger into his
right eye; your thumb may be
under his jaw or nose.

Bend the attacker over backwards across your right knee by exerting pressure with your right hand to his eye and face.

Lift your left elbow high.

Strike down sharply with the right elbow to the attacker's solar plexis.

177

When your arms are grabbed by two persons . . .

lift your right leg to a parallel position to the floor and bend slightly at the knee.

Extend and lock the right leg out, driving the heel of your foot (shoe) into the chest or solar plexis of one attacker.

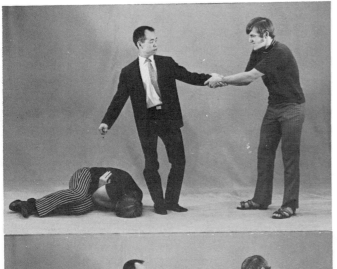

Pull the second attacker toward you.

Lift the left leg and deliver a side kick to the second person.

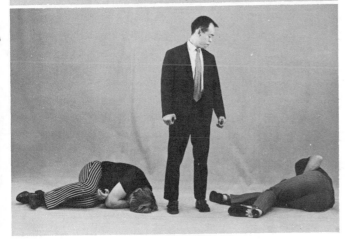

You are in position to refocus your attention to the first person, if necessary, or to leave.

179

When an attacker grabs you with one hand by the lapel . . .

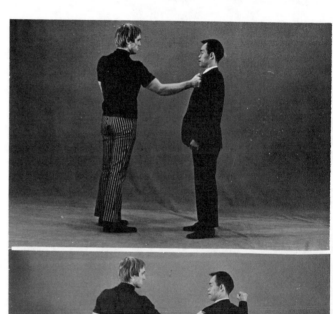

bring your right arm back with the forearm perpendicular to the ground and palm facing forward.

Stepping in with the right foot, pivot the body sharply, bringing your right arm around in order to hit your attacker's forearm with your wrist.

Continue your arm around so that your fist is at your back shoulder.

Thrust your right elbow forward as you shift your weight forward to deliver an elbow blow to the midsection or solar plexis.

181

When grabbed by the lapel with one hand you can also . . .

place your left hand on top of your attacker's and your right hand on top of your own left. Hold the attacker's hand firmly against your body.

Step back with your right foot.

Bend your knees and squat straight down. Do not bend your body forward.

When attacked by two persons, one from behind and the other in front . . .

wait until the person facing you begins his move toward you, then instantly bring your right foot up and forward with a front kick, driving the toe of your foot (shoe) into his midsection.

Bring your right foot back down between the feet of the person holding you from behind. Quickly pivot your body to the left, moving your left foot out and assuming a horseback stance. While you are pivoting, raise your left arm sharply and pull your right arm to your side with your fist clenched tight.

Drive your right fist straight upward to the jaw of the second person.

183

PICTORIAL

About Face
DUIRO DORA
A turn of 180°.

At Ease
SHEER
From a ready stance, move only arms and hands to side; relax; feet remain in same position.

Attention
CHARYO
Heels and toes together with arms and hands at side, looking straight ahead.

Back Fist
YIKWON

Back Stance
FUGUL
Feet form 90° angle; 30 percent of body weight on front foot, the foot moved, and 70 percent on back, the stationary foot.

GLOSSARY

Begin
SHEJAK
Command to start training.

Breaking
KYOKPA
The act of breaking material (wood, cinder blocks, etc.) as a demonstration of power.

Elbow
PALKUMCHI

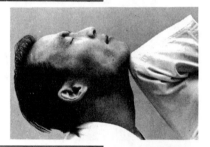

End
GOMAN
The command to conclude training; student should go to ready parallel (CHUNBI) stance.

Fixed Stance
KOCHUNG SOGI
Similar to back stance, but body weight is evenly distributed.

Forearm
PALMOK
Outer wrist, unless otherwise specified.

Free Sparring
JAYU TAERYON
No-contact sparring training between students in order to practice techniques and discipline.

Front Snap Kick
AP CHAGI

Front Stance
CHONGUL
Both feet pointed forward, back leg locked, front knee bent; 70 percent of body weight on front foot and 30 percent on back foot.

Gymnasium
DOJANG
Specific place for Tae Kwon Do training.

Heel
BAL TWIKUMCHI

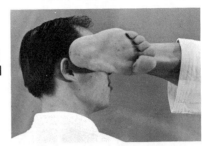

High
SANGDAN

Facial area; more specifically, the center of the face.

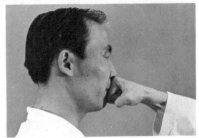

Inner Wrist
ANPALMOK

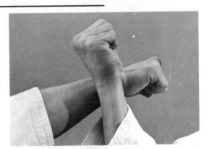

Knee
MURUP

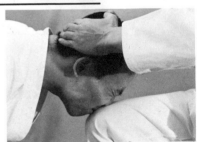

Knife Hand
SUDO

Hand is open, flat, tensed; fingers are together and slightly bent.

187

Knife Hand Strike
SUDO TAERIGI
Strike with fleshy part of outer hand.

Left
CHWA or WEN

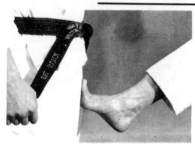

Low
HARDAN
Groin area.

Middle
CHUNGDAN
Solar plexus area.

One-Step Sparring
ILBO TAERYON
Limited sparring technique for practicing exact movements of Tae Kwon Do techniques.

Overturn Punch
TWICHIBO CHIRUGI
Punch in which the back of the fist is down.

Palm Heel
CHANGKWON
The base of the palm. The palm heel punch is a punch using the base of the palm with the thumb and fingers curled to avoid injury.

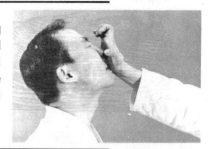

Punch
CHIRUGI
Straight punch, unless otherwise specified.

Ready
CHUNBI
Stance at beginning or conclusion of training; feet slightly apart, fists in front of body, waist high about 1" from knot of belt and 1" apart.

Reverse Knife Hand
YOK SUDO
Edge of hand along the index finger. Commonly known as "ridge hand".

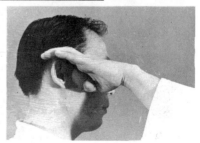

Reverse Punch
PANDAE CHIRUGI
Punch with hand opposite front foot; e.g., right fist punch with left foot forward, and vice versa.

Riding Stance
KIMA SOGI
Horseback riding stance; feet pointing forward; knees bent; straight posture.

Right
WOO or ORUN

Rising Block
CHUKYO MARKI
Rising block always performed with outer wrist and from front stance.

Roundhouse Kick
TOLYO CHAGI
A kick with the ball or instep of the foot while pivoting the body.

Salute
KYUNGYE

A bow to flag, instructor or fellow student.

Side Block
YOP MARKI

Inner wrist block from back stance.

Side Thrust Kick
YOP CHAGI

Perhaps most effective, useful kick in Tae Kwon Do in which contact is made with heel which is thrust to the side.

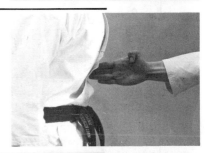

Spear Finger
KWANSU

Fingertip attack either vertically or horizontally; fingers tensed, even.

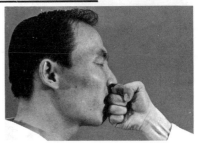

Vertical Punch
SEWO CHIRUGI

Punch in which the back of the fist is vertical.

KOREAN COUNTING

1	HANA	1st	ILL
2	DOOL	2nd	YEE
3	SET	3rd	SAM
4	NET	4th	SAH
5	TASUT	5th	OH
6	YAUSUT	6th	YOOK
7	ILGOPE	7th	CHIL
8	YAUDUL	8th	PAL
9	AHOPE	9th	KOO
10	YAUL	10th	SHIB
100	BAIK	100th	BAIK
1,000	CHUN	1,000th	CHUN
10,000	MAHN	10,000th	MAHN